Learn To Juggle In 15 Minutes

3 Ball Juggling for adults & kids

D1534664

J A CRAWSHAW

Published by Xylem Publishing

The 3 ball system can be achieved in 15 minutes or less, but the reading of this book may take longer.

Cover image by Shutter stock
Cover design by J A Crawshaw
Images by Lewis Jordan

Introduction

Congratulations, you've taken the first steps to becoming a juggler.

Juggling is a fantastic skill to have. Whether you are juggling alone, with friends, or as part of a club, juggling is truly international and unites people from all over the world.

You will become part of a unique group of very talented people.

By following the eight steps within this book and paying particular attention to the hints and tips, you could be juggling within 15 minutes. This book is designed to introduce you to the three ball cascade system and learn all the practical moves in 15 minutes, but I recommend you read the entire book first.

The book covers more detail, including troubleshooting issues and advice on where to find more information, juggling four balls and more.

Juggling is a skill which needs practice, and the more you practice, the better you will become, that's a guarantee. One of my greatest tips for anyone learning for the first time is not to get frustrated if you're not progressing as quickly as you want. Instead, take your time and persevere. You are training your brain to do something it's never done before and that takes a little patience. One thing is for sure, the results can be mind-blowing.

A Bit About The Author

John Crawshaw has been juggling since he was about 10 years old, when he picked fruit out of the fruit bowl and taught himself. He cost his mum a fortune in bruised apples and oranges, but progressed to balls as a teenager. Joining the Cosmos Juggling Club in York, England in 1992, where he learned to juggle clubs, knives and perform tricks with other jugglers. He set up the university juggling club at The University of Humberside and performed on an amateur basis at fetes and fundraising events.

To earn extra money, while at university, he taught people on the street to juggle in 15 minutes and that's where the inspiration for this book came from.

A sufferer of dyslexia, he found juggling to be an immense help to his brain, when often he would become stressed or confused. Juggling somehow managed to help. In 2021 at the age of 52 he wrote 'The Void Between Words', his memoir and personal journey of battling with dyslexia and associated mental health issues. Juggling features significantly within the book and is highly recommended if you want to find out more about how juggling can help you with learning difficulties and focussing your brain. (Link at the end of this book).

He is not a professional juggler, but juggling has remained a hobby to which he is very grateful. He hopes this book might at least introduce you to the wonderful world of juggling, but moreover, encourage you to see that you could acquire a new skill, and that anything is possible.

Follow each step within the book carefully. Don't be frightened of going back to an earlier stage if you feel you need to. In fact, this is my greatest advice of all, and all the people I have taught have done better and progressed more quickly when they routinely go back to the previous step and nail it before moving on.

Okay, let's get straight to it.

8 Reasons Why Juggling Is Good For You

1. Juggling boosts brain development. Research indicates that learning to juggle accelerates the growth of neural connections related to memory, focus, movement, and vision. The beneficial changes persist even after weeks without practice.

2. Juggling doesn't discriminate by age, size, gender, race, religion or athletic ability. Anyone can be a fantastic juggler.

3. Juggling builds hand-eye coordination in ways that improve reaction time, reflexes, spatial awareness, strategic thinking, and concentration. This helps improve confidence as well as athletic ability. It may, also, even promote reading skills

4. Juggling gets you moving enough to increase your oxygen intake.

5. Juggling can be stimulating as well as calming. While learning more complicated juggling skills you rely on left-brain processes, carefully focusing and analysing the steps. When practicing skills you've

already mastered you rely on right-brained processes, relaxing into a more fluid, intuitive motion. The bringing together of both sides, can be a very powerful thing.

6. Juggling puts you in charge, since you can make it as easy or difficult as you choose. Start with three balls. To ramp up the challenge increase the speed, add more balls, or change patterns. You can also change props, learn trick juggling, try multi-person juggling or go for the chainsaws!

7. Juggling teaches a growth mindset. You learn from mistakes, noticing how effort and increasing experience bring you ever greater mastery.

8. Juggling is incredible fun.

Step 1. Let's Get Started

What will you need? One of the great things about juggling is that all you need is a bit of space and something to juggle with. It doesn't have to be an expensive hobby. Although I don't advocate going straight for the chainsaws, three objects which you can throw and catch comfortably are perfect. I started juggling as a young boy with random items of fruit from the fruit bowl, using oranges and apples and the occasional banana to make things a little more difficult. Specific juggling balls are perfect and an excellent investment. Not only do they feel good to throw and catch, but they look good too. My advice would be to get them from a juggling supplies shop, where they tend to be more heavier weighted than some cheaper versions. Feeling the definite thud of the ball in your hand makes the process much easier. But it's your personal choice.

At this stage, we are going to forget about the balls. It's tempting to hold all three balls in your hands and try to juggle them into the air. Like any other sport or activity, attaining the correct position and stance will help you greatly to achieve good results.

It's important to adopt a good stance right at the beginning. Put the balls to one side and stand with your feet shoulder width apart so that you are comfortable and relaxed.

Flex slightly at the knees and keep your back straight. As usual with all beginners, there is a tendency to throw the balls forward and flexing at the knees and keeping your back straight will help to prevent this from happening. This doesn't mean that you are bending over at the knees, but just flexing in a relaxed style, like on a skate or surf board. In fact, being relaxed is the key to success with juggling, and if you find yourself becoming too tense and rigid, then just stop, take time out and start again when you are ready.

Now, before we bring any balls into the situation, I want you to hold your hands out with your elbows at 90° as if you were holding a tray or similar. Again, they should be shoulder width apart. It's important to keep your wrists up so that your hands are level with your arms, don't let your hands drop down at the wrists.

Remember to breathe. In my opinion. breathing is one of the keys to success, It's tempting when learning a new skill to hold your breath until you've mastered it, but

breathing in a relaxed fashion again will help you to achieve quicker and better results. What you will find, hopefully, is that the process of juggling in itself will help you to relax and your breathing will be calm. But to start off, be conscious of your breathing.

Step 2. First Ball

Now take one ball and hold it in your dominant hand. This is usually the hand you would use to write with, but you may feel comfortable with the opposite? It's up to you and do whatever feels natural.

1 ball

Holding the ball in that hand and I want you to imagine a triangle in front of you. A triangle which is flat along the bottom with your hands at each end. The triangle will go up to a point in front of you, with the point just above your head height. This is the pattern the balls will be thrown in, so it's important to visualise it. The balls will pivot at the same point at the top of the triangle and then descend down into each corner where your hands will be waiting.

Now throw the ball up into the air so that it goes to the point of the triangle and then down to your other hand and catch it. In truth, the ball doesn't actually go to a

Triangle

point but a more rounded point, so if you can imagine a triangle with a rounded top, that's more accurate.

The aim is not to rush things. You need enough time to be able to get the other balls into play. There is a sweet spot which is not too low and not too high which will enable you to juggle with three balls effortlessly. Too low and there will not be enough time to introduce the other balls. Too high and there is a danger of losing

control and aim. The ball should just go to above head height.

Return the ball to your dominant hand. We will call this 'hand one' and your other, 'hand two'. With the ball in hand one, throw it so that it pivots at the top just above head height and then drops down into hand two and stop there.

Hints & tips for this section are not to raise your hands too high. They shouldn't go higher than chest height and, ideally, around waist height. In addition, when you catch, try to follow through as if you are almost cushioning the fall. This will help later, when you have to throw it again to create a more continuous fluid action.

Return the ball to hand one and practise throwing to hand two and repeat this until it feels comfortable. It's important not to be tempted to rush into two or three balls at this stage, but to work on the one ball technique until you feel confident.

Now when you are comfortable catching the ball in hand two, throw the ball from hand two back to hand one, so that the ball pivots at the same place at the top of the triangle and then catch the ball in hand one. This may feel a little strange, as your dominant hand will feel more natural starting, but if you can master this move, then you have cracked juggling. Seriously! Because this is the only move you will need to do, to juggle one ball, three balls, five balls, seven balls etc. Getting this right from the start opens the gate for you to be a competent juggler.

Again, practise this move over and over until you achieve a smooth rhythm.

Your eyes should try to see the whole triangle, but mainly concentrate on the pivot point. What you don't want to be doing is focussing tightly on the ball. As I said, try to see the whole picture.

At this point, you might not feel like you've made much progress, but really you should congratulate yourself. Because this is the only thing you need to do to juggle three balls and you have established the fundamentals to moving forward to STEP 3. WELL DONE!

Step 3. Introducing The Second Ball

Now take a ball in hand one and another ball in hand two. Throw ball 1 from hand one as you have been doing in the previous step, making sure it pivots at the top of the triangle and then drops down to hand two. Just before you catch it, you release ball 2 up to the pivot point and then catch it with hand one.

The tip here is to make sure that the outgoing ball goes underneath the incoming ball and not outside it, and time it so that they don't collide. Don't throw too early. In reality, you leave it almost to the last second, before you release.

Don't worry if you don't catch every ball, this is common and again practice will make perfect. Go through the process again and again, making sure that you keep your wrists up and that both balls pivot at the same point at the top of the triangle. This is where you can start to count to create a rhythm.

'One and two'. Count out loud as you throw and catch the balls. Throw ball 1 as you say 'one,' throw ball 2 and simultaneously catch ball 1 as you say 'and' then catch ball 2 as you say 'two'.

The tip here is to count as slowly as you possibly can. The balls will dictate the pace to some degree, but trying to control the rhythm by saying it as slowly as possible will give you more time when it comes to ball number 3 later on.

Repeat this step until you are fluid. This is a critical stage, because most people feel the urge to get hold of the third ball and try introducing it to the pattern. Don't. Stick with two balls and practise this move until your brain is happy with it.

Hints & tips here are not to rush. Keep counting and the slower you can go, the better, trust me.

If you are experiencing passing the balls between hands to create a circular pattern, stop and reload. This is a style of juggling, and the typical 'clown style' you might see. But it's a dead end if you want to progress to clubs, knives and more balls etc. and actually much, much harder. If this is you, it will be difficult to break the pattern in your brain, particularly if you did this many years ago as a child or at school. I have seen people break this pattern in a 100% of cases, so it is possible.

Step 4. Two Ball Juggling

Congratulations. If you are at this point, you are doing very well and are so close to pulling this off.

Start as you did in STEP 3 and this time, when you catch ball 2, throw it again immediately as if you are repeating the original pattern and it becomes ball 1. Keep this going so that you are effectively two ball juggling. Remember to count, 'one and two... one and two... one and two'. See how long you can keep going.

The tip here is to keep things slow and make sure both balls go to the same height.

Step 5. Breaking Barriers

At this stage, your brain may have gone through some tough challenges, or you may be one of the lucky ones who instinctively can feel the rhythm? Either way, you are well on your way to being a juggler. In fact, I would say, there is really no looking back now as you progress to this stage.

What we are going to do now is repeat Step 4, but start with hand two. This is not always an easy step.

Your brain may take some convincing, but we've been here before with one ball, so you know what to do. I want you to count 'two and one... two and one... two and one'.

Throw on 'two' and catch and throw on 'and' then catch on 'one'.

As before, practise this until you are fluid.

The tip here is to make sure your catches are solid. As always, if you're not quite feeling it, go back to one ball in Step 1 and polish that move and then move steadily through Steps 2 to 6 when you feel comfortable.

Step 6. Bringing It All Together

With a ball in each hand, start with your dominant hand, as you have done before. Now, every time you are about to make a catch, release the ball in that hand and continue the pattern.

'One and two... two and one...one and two...two and one etc.'

Effectively, what you are doing is starting with your dominant hand and completing two catches. Then stop briefly and start again with your less dominant hand and complete two catches. Then repeat the sequence.

You should feel more confident that both hands are throwing the balls to the same height and making solid catches. You are now two ball juggling and the hard bit has been done.

Now for three balls!

Step 7. You're Nearly There

Take two balls in hand one and one ball in hand two.

At this point, we won't do anything with ball 3. We're just going to get used to having it around. Start with ball 1 and repeat what we have done previously, by throwing ball 1 and then ball 2 and catch them in sequence. This won't be easy, as you have ball 3 in your hand. There's nothing new here, in terms of the throws and catches, just as we did in Steps 5 and 6, except there is another ball in hand one, which makes the catch more difficult.

Do it again and this time, eject ball 3 from your hand as you go to catch ball 2. It doesn't matter where it goes. Drop it, throw it up or over your shoulder, just get rid of it, so that your hand is free to make the catch. It might feel natural to throw it into the mix? If so, do it,

but there is no need at this point if you're concentrating on just freeing up your hand for the catch.

Pick up the balls and repeat this move.
If it helps, and I still do this after 40 years of juggling, say the rhyme, 'one and two'. Eject ball 3 as you say 'two' and catch incoming ball 2.

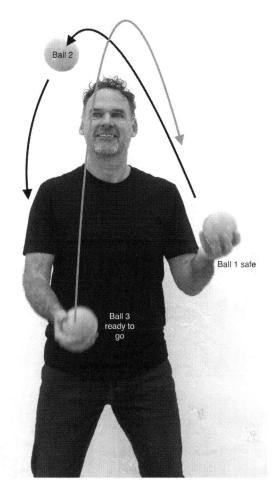

If you're really feeling it and have thrown ball 3 into the mix. Brilliant! Just keep going.

The tip here is to keep practising this move. It's common at this point to rush. Keep the timing as slow as possible, 'one and two'.

Step 8. The Big One!

Stop for a minute and contemplate how far you have come. You are doing incredibly well and the next step is not as hard as you might think.

In fact, the next step is nothing new! You are not actually doing anything different to what you have done in Step 1. Ball 3 is really just another ball 1. You throw it exactly as you do ball 1, from your dominant hand, to pivot at the same height as balls 1 and 2 and then catch it.

Take a breath, keep your back straight and flex at the knees.
You can do this.
Timing is everything here, and what you have done in the previous steps will have prepared you well if you have kept things as slow as possible. If you find you haven't enough time to fit ball 3 in, you're not throwing the balls high enough or your hands have crept up slightly.
If you think you need more time? Go back through the previous steps and slow things down to create more time.
Ok. With two balls in your dominant hand and one ball in the other, start your first throw. Don't feel intimidated. You can do this, believe in yourself and see

the pattern in front of you. Remember, there's nothing new now.

Ball 1 is thrown to the pivot point.
Just before you catch ball 1, you throw ball 2.
Just before you catch ball 2, you throw ball 3 and just before you catch it, you throw the ball which is in that hand so you can make a solid catch.

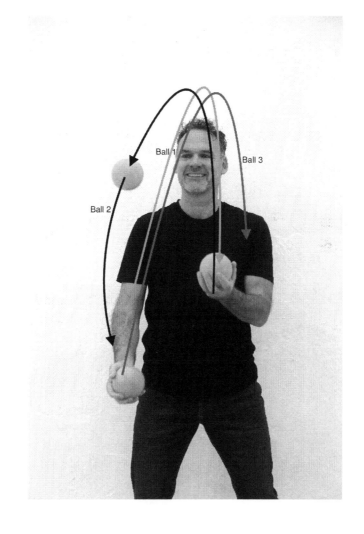

Most people at this stage drop this ball and that's natural. It feels so completely mad that you have just juggled.

Yes! You have just juggled three balls. Boom! You're a juggler.

The tip here is to make a solid catch of ball 3 and don't worry too much about catching ball 4. This will come. Remember, you've done it before.

You have now completed all eight steps and know everything you need to juggle three balls. Keep practising and don't be afraid of going back a step. People who go back to refresh a previous step, tend to progress quicker in the long run. It's actually worth the time investment, even if it feels like a backwards step.

Keep practising this step and when you feel ready, release each ball just before you make each catch. The trick now, it to make it continuous. If you do? You're juggling. You've done it!

It's such a fantastic feeling. Congratulate yourself. The hard work paid off.

Well done.

Troubleshooting

Problem	Reason	Things to try
Walking forward	You're walking forward because you're throwing the balls slightly forward in the pattern.	Don't hunch forwards Don't let your wrists drop Try juggling close to a wall
Breaking concentration due to picking the balls off the floor	Breaking your stance and concentration as you routinely pick up balls is common	Try juggling next to a bed or sofa. Now the balls are more easily reached
Missing a solid catch	The balls are bouncing off or missing your hand	Avoid balls which are too big or too small. Balls specifically for juggling are soft but weighted. These might help. Where you look is vital. Concentrate on the whole picture and not the catches specifically
Not enough time to get ball 3 into the mix	Balls 1 and 2 are moving too quickly	Throw the balls higher to create more time. Don't go too high though, as you might lose control. Leave the throw of the outgoing ball to the last minute

Chasing the balls	Inconsistent throws	This is very common and I still do this today. Try concentrating on the pivot point and get every ball to the same point. Keep your body aligned and your hands level with each other
Passing balls between hands instead of throwing	Your brain has been conditioned to this style	Start at step 1 and focus on throwing the ball from hand to hand
Can't seem to progress	There may be many reasons	Rushing and wanting to progress faster than you are able is very common. Slow down and don't be afraid to invest in going back to a previous step. You may be in the wrong environment. Find somewhere quiet and with space. Try to think about juggling and nothing else
Feeling mentally & physically exhausted	It is possible to overdo it! Juggling can involve huge shifts in thinking and physical activity	Take a break and don't think you have to be a competent juggler the first time you do it. Often taking breaks and coming back to it fresh helps you progress faster

Reflecting And Moving On

The freedom of continual juggling can be an extremely exhilarating experience. Let your mind enjoy the process. You might find that it becomes so natural that you can switch off to everything around you and use juggling to relax and even meditate.

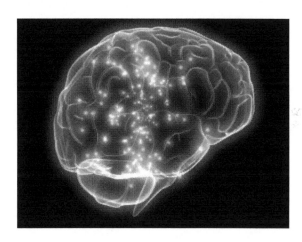

The more you improve, the easier it will become, and you will stop focussing on throwing and catching and more on the holistic pattern. In a way, it becomes instinctive, like riding a bike or driving a car.

It's been proven that juggling can bring together both sides of the brain and, in doing so, allows your brain to relax. It feels great, and I know many people who use juggling to relax, clear their thoughts and even meditate. As I do.

This could be very useful, before an important exam or interview or if you're just feeling stressed or anxious. At the end of the day, juggling is a fun thing to do. Enjoy your juggling and see where it takes you.
You could even make a career out of it.

No matter how good you become, dropping the balls is something that will always happen, so don't beat yourself up about it. Street entertainers and performers actually incorporate a drop into part of the show if it happens. Or, they simply pick it up and continue without making a big fuss. Believe me, people who can't juggle will be impressed anyway.

Enjoy your juggling. You're now in a very unique club. The world is your oyster and balls are just the start. Try moving on to juggling with clubs, rings or even fire! There are groups and societies where you can get further guidance. I wouldn't recommend going straight out and investing in some fire clubs without further training, but there are endless possibilities. There are also many other books which go into much more detail and even scientific study into the health benefits and cognitive effects of juggling if you want to delve deeper. This book is designed to introduce you to the wonderful world of juggling and not an attempt to blind you with science, but it's out there if you want it.

There are also many social media groups and juggling influencers, who offer more detailed information and ideas. Best of all, there is nothing better than getting together with other jugglers and exchanging ideas and experiences. It has happened to me all over the world, from beaches to nightclubs, where someone spotted me juggling or vice versa. You never know. You might be able to teach someone else with your new-found skill.

Enjoy!

Juggling With More Balls!

You might have zoomed through this book so quickly and easily that you are already thinking about juggling with more balls?

This, of course, can be done. With the same amount of practice and determination, anything is possible. One piece of advice, though, is that the pattern changes depending on the number.

The triangle pattern in this book is perfect for three balls and five balls, but how do you fit four balls in? You might have tried to think about how that is possible, and wished you had another hand?

In fact, the pattern is completely different, as it is for most even-numbered ball routines. Instead of a triangle, you are working within a square. Start with two balls in each hand, and each two ball set, stay in the same hand. The balls from each hand never cross and just go up and down in pairs. The trick is to fool the eye into thinking it's more complicated, by throwing the balls at different intervals, so that they are out of sync. It looks impressive, and it's quick. But remember the earlier steps of this book and establish a good stance, breath and take your time. There are other books and videos for this technique which may help you to progress.

Juggling With Clubs

Once you have mastered juggling with three balls, the same principal can be used for juggling other items such as rings, scarves and clubs.

The pattern is just the same as with three balls, but this time you are catching the handle of each club. As you throw, your hand initiates a rotation of the club, so that it spins one whole revolution, before it is caught. The tip of the club (the opposite end to the handle) rotates towards you until the handle ends in its original position, but in the other hand.

Again, the outgoing club goes underneath the incoming. The key to success is to create time, just as you did with the balls and to point the clubs at 45^0 to your body and not 90^0 This will feel more natural and avoid collisions.

More Information

The Complete Juggler by Dave Finnigan
Juggling With Finesse by Kit Summers

International Jugglers Association.
https://www.juggle.org

European Juggling Association.
https://www.eja.net

My memoir 'The Void Between Words' can be found on Amazon, in bookstores and other digital platforms. Find

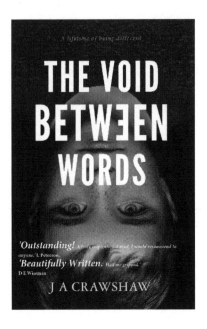

out how juggling helped me to overcome my learning difficulties.

https://www.amazon.co.uk/dp/183837731X

https://www.amazon.com/Void-Between-Words-lifetime-different/dp/183837731X

If you have found this book useful? I would be incredibly grateful if you would spare two minutes to write a review on the relevant platform.

Good reviews help others access the book and help us to spread the positivity and health benefits of juggling to others.

Instagram: J_A_Crawshaw_Author

Made in the USA
Monee, IL
16 December 2021

85947401R00024